MATT CHRISTOPHER

On the Field with . . .
Terrell Davis

MATT CHRISTOPHER

On the Field with ...
Terrell Davis

Little, Brown and Company

Boston   New York   London

Copyright © 2000 by Catherine M. Christopher

First Edition

Cover photograph by John Iacono, *Sports Illustrated*/©Time Inc.

Library of Congress Cataloging-in-Publication Data

Christopher, Matt.
    On the field with . . . Terrell Davis / Matt Christopher. — 1st ed.
       p. cm.
    Summary: A biography of the Denver Broncos running back who helped his team to two consecutive Super Bowl titles in 1998 and 1999.
    ISBN 0-316-13552-6
    1. Davis, Terrell, 1972–   Juvenile literature.   2. Football players — United States Biography Juvenile literature.   3. Denver Broncos (Football team) Juvenile literature. [1. Davis, Terrell, 1972–   .
2. Football players.   3. Afro-Americans Biography.]   I. Title.
GV939.D349C57   2000
796.323'092 — dc21
[B]   99-41273

10 9 8 7 6 5 4 3 2 1

COM-MO

Printed in the United States of America

Contents

MATT CHRISTOPHER

On the Field with . . .
Terrell Davis

Chapter One:
1972–1987

Boss Hogg

Denver Bronco Terrell Davis is not the biggest running back in the National Football League. In an era when many running backs weigh 250 pounds or more, Davis weighs just over two hundred pounds. He is also not the fastest or shiftiest running back in the league. But he is, without a doubt, the most determined. That's why he is also the best running back in professional football today, and one of the best ever.

Terrell Davis has overcome obstacles that would have sidetracked most other players. He grew up in a family devastated by problems with alcohol, crime, and drugs. Though he was on football teams throughout his childhood, in high school, where most future pro players start honing their skills, he didn't play until his junior year. After graduation, few colleges thought he had the ability to play big-time football. Then, when he was set to play on a college team, the college he enrolled in dropped its football program. After transferring to another school, he was a second-string player beset by injuries.

Still, he was good enough to catch the notice of the pros. In 1995, he was picked in the sixth round of the NFL draft by the Denver Broncos. He was given little chance to make the team, yet he managed to work his way up from the sixth string to become the starting running back. A year later, despite a series of injuries and the debilitating effects of migraine headaches, he was recognized as one of the best backs in the league. In the 1997–98 season, he led the NFL in rushing and was named the MVP of the Super Bowl, while in 1998–99, he nearly set an all-time rushing record and led the Broncos to another Super Bowl win.

Terrell Davis hasn't allowed anything to stop him. As he once told a reporter, "I know good things happen to you and bad things happen to you. My motto is to expect the unexpected — and that life goes on."

While he was growing up, no one ever would have expected that he would become one of the greatest players in professional football. But Terrell Davis has proven that a person can overcome just about any obstacle through hard work and determination.

In the Davis family, that's something of a tradition. His parents, Joe and Kataree Davis, both grew up in St. Louis, Missouri. Neither came from a wealthy family. Kataree lived with her grandparents while her mother studied nursing. Joe, meanwhile, grew up on the streets. His parents neglected him. His mother was a heavy drinker and his father often beat him.

As a teenager Joe was in and out of trouble. On several occasions he was sent to juvenile detention centers for committing petty crimes, and he even served time in jail after being involved in a robbery. Yet Joe wasn't bad: he just made a lot of bad decisions.

Kataree was sixteen years old in August of 1964 when she met nineteen-year-old Joe Davis at a party. Although her mother didn't approve of the relationship, the couple soon became inseparable.

After Kataree became pregnant, the two married in April of 1965. A few months later, their first child, Joe Jr., was born.

Life was hard for the young couple. Joe had a menial job in a factory and money was tight. When Kataree became pregnant again, he began looking for another way to make money.

He found what he thought was an easy way out, taking part in another robbery. But he was caught and sent to jail for three years. Kataree moved in with a girlfriend, and after her second son, James, was born, she went to work in a factory to support her family. She was only eighteen years old.

Kataree Davis was determined to keep her family together, and through her own hard work, she succeeded. When Joe got out of jail in 1969, they resumed their life together. By 1971, the family included three more sons, Reggie, Robert, and Terry.

Kataree's grandparents had moved to San Diego, California, and wrote her that life was better in California than Missouri. St. Louis was a southern city, and despite advances in civil rights, there were few opportunities at that time for African Americans to get good jobs. Conditions were better in San Diego.

With another child on the way, Kataree Davis saved her money, packed up all their belongings in a trunk, and took her five young children to San Diego by bus. One month after they arrived, Joe Davis joined his family in California. A few days later, on October 28, 1972, Terrell Davis was born.

For the first few months of his life, little Terrell was sick. He just couldn't keep any food down. No matter how often he was fed, he had a hard time gaining weight.

The Davises couldn't afford to spend much money taking him to doctors. They finally discovered he could eat strained carrots. He began gaining weight, then eventually outgrew whatever was wrong with him. When he did, his mother went to work as a nurse's aide and began attending college part-time, studying nursing. Joe Davis was having a hard time holding a steady job, and she wanted to make sure she would always be able to provide for her children.

Then Joe Davis was arrested again, on a reckless

driving charge. Because of his record, he was sent back to prison. Terrell's mother still managed to keep working, going to school, and raising her children. She even saved enough money to buy a house.

When Joe got out of prison in 1976, things got better for the Davis family. For the first time, the family was stable. They all did their share. Although he was only five years old, Terrell even got his first job, delivering newspapers, a job he kept until his sophomore year of high school. Every morning he woke at 4:30 to put the papers together, then went out into his neighborhood on his bicycle to deliver them before dawn. "That's what kept me in good shape," he said years later, "riding my bike up those steep hills. Throwing those Sunday papers, that's like lifting weights."

In 1979 the family moved into a brand-new five-bedroom home. The future was beginning to look bright.

That same year, when he was seven, Terrell started playing football. The new house was right around the corner from the park where the local Pop Warner football league played.

He joined his older brother Terry on the Bucca-

neers. Both boys played offensive guard, and they loved competing with one another each game to see who could make the best blocks. Joe Davis went to almost every game and practice with his sons, cheering them on from the sidelines. Terrell played baseball and basketball, too, but he liked football best of all.

Then one day after a game, a frightening thing happened. Terrell was waiting for his mother to pick him up, when all of a sudden, he had trouble seeing. By the time his mother arrived, he was almost blind.

His vision soon returned, but when it did he got a searing headache. Nothing his mother did could stop the pain pounding in his head like a sledgehammer. Hours later, his head still throbbing, Terrell cried himself to sleep.

When he awoke later that night, the pain had miraculously disappeared. But for the rest of his childhood, every three or four weeks he would be plagued by a terrible headache. He had no idea what caused them. Whenever they happened, Terrell would just sit as still as possible in a dark room and suffer silently.

In 1980, the relationship between Terrell's parents deteriorated. Joe Davis just couldn't stay out of trouble. Although he was working as a welder, he was drinking heavily, and there was evidence that he was selling marijuana. In fact, Terrell remembers finding marijuana around the house.

There were times, too, when Joe seemed to be following in his own father's abusive footsteps. He was violent toward his family, striking them and even threatening them with guns. But at the same time, he was strict with his sons, made certain they knew he loved them, and did the best he could. Still, conditions were hard.

At last, Kataree Davis and her husband separated. The two oldest boys, Joe Jr. and James, stayed with Kataree. Terrell and the other three younger boys went to live with their father, although they usually spent the weekends back with their mother. Joe Davis lived in a poor, Hispanic neighborhood. The Davis boys were virtually the only African-American children in the area. They didn't have many friends and often got into fights on their way to and from school.

As crazy as things got at home, Terrell was just a

young boy who loved his parents and tried to do the best he could.

In his second season of Pop Warner football, Terrell's coach, Frank White, noticed that eight-year-old Terrell had grown bigger and become faster. He moved him from guard to running back.

Terrell loved running with the football. In his first game in the backfield he ran for several long touchdowns. He liked the attention he got after a good run, when the fans cheered and his teammates patted him on the back. Coach White nicknamed him "Boss Hogg" after a character on a television show, and soon everyone in the neighborhood was calling Terrell Boss. Such recognition for his achievements made Terrell feel good about himself.

Word soon spread among the other coaches in the league that the young boy everyone called Boss was almost impossible to stop. To try to throw off the opposition, Coach White had Terrell wear a different jersey for every game so the other team couldn't tell which player was "the Boss" by looking at his number. But as soon as Terrell touched the football, they quickly figured out who he was. He was the boy with the football, running for touchdowns. Terrell didn't bother trying to avoid tacklers — he just ran over them.

Football became the outlet for Terrell's emotions. No matter how bad things were at home, there was always a football game to look forward to.

And at home, things soon went from bad to worse. Terrell's father got into an argument with a friend, and the man came to Joe Davis's house with a gun. Instead of calling the police, Joe Davis decided to defend himself with his own gun. In a matter of moments, the argument escalated into gunfire.

Terrell awoke to find a policeman pointing a gun at his head. While the boys were sleeping, Joe Davis had shot his friend. Although the other man wasn't badly hurt, a neighbor heard the shooting and called the police. Joe Davis was arrested and sent back to prison.

With his father gone, football became even more important to Terrell. In his second season playing running back, he was even better than he had been before. One of his mother's friends promised him five dollars for every touchdown he scored, thinking he might get one or two a game. But Terrell usually scored four or five and was making twenty or twenty-five dollars a game, enough to take the team out for ice cream and other treats.

But football alone couldn't replace his father or keep Terrell out of trouble. He looked to his older brothers for guidance. But the two oldest boys, Joe and James, were in the military and usually out of touch. Reggie was busy playing high school football. Robert and Terry were already getting into trouble themselves.

The boys did the best they could to keep Terrell, the baby of the family, clear of serious trouble, but they were teenagers themselves. Terrell didn't become a bad kid, but he started to drift, spending time just hanging out, breakdancing with his friends, skateboarding, and getting into the usual sort of mischief many young boys do.

Terrell's father finally got out of prison and rejoined the family. The next few years were good, but just as Terrell began ninth grade, Joe Davis became ill. Doctors diagnosed a disease called lupus, a disorder of the immune system that causes the body to attack its own connective tissues and organs.

At the same time, Terrell stopped playing football. It's the rule in Pop Warner football that players not exceed a certain weight, so no one has a big advantage because of his size. But Terrell was growing up. By the time he was ready to enter ninth grade, despite trying to keep his weight down by jogging in a sweat suit, Terrell had outgrown Pop Warner football. While he had always been a star in Pop Warner ball, as a ninth grader, he was small for high school football. He was too intimidated to try out for the team at Morse High School and began to drift away from the game.

Terrell felt lost at Morse from the first day of ninth grade. Most students came from families who had more money than his, and Terrell felt self-conscious. He was also worried about his father's health. Without football to focus on, he began to withdraw into a shell.

At first, he went to school every day, but he couldn't concentrate and soon fell behind on his work. Then, embarrassed to be so far behind, he started skipping school entirely, preferring to ride around by himself on his white motor scooter. He was soon failing every class.

That same year, Joe Davis, weakened from years of alcohol abuse and failure to take care of himself, was admitted to the hospital. A few days later, Terrell and some of his brothers were at a park playing a game of pickup baseball. A family friend drove up and told the boys their mother wanted them to go to the hospital.

The boys all piled into the car and met their mother at the hospital. As soon as she saw them, she began to cry.

Joe Davis was dying. The boys met with their father one last time, just long enough to give him a hug. A short time later, on April 17, 1987, Joe Davis died.

Terrell Davis was fourteen years old.

Chapter Two:
1987–1990

Nose to the Grindstone

As Kataree Davis remembered later, Joe Davis's death "affected all the children." Her older sons became more responsible, while the younger boys got a little wild. Terrell later said his father's death "hardened" him. He had always been happy-go-lucky, but now he was morose and withdrawn. When he returned to Morse for his sophomore year of high school in the fall of 1987, he felt more alone than ever.

He'd lost interest in just about everything. He'd once been a good student but was now so far behind he felt that the situation was hopeless.

But his mother wouldn't let him quit. She got angry with him and let him know that he was disappointing her. That made Terrell feel bad, because he was beginning to realize just how hard his mother

14

had been working to keep the family together. Nearly every day she woke between four and five o'clock in the morning to prepare the evening meal, then went off to work, often taking double shifts to earn extra money. She was a giving person and was always taking less fortunate friends and relatives into her home. Terrell didn't want to let his mother down.

He sensed he was in trouble. Without an education, he knew it would be almost impossible to get a good job. For a while, he tried to work harder at school, but he got frustrated easily. He felt as if all the teachers thought he was a poor student and not worth the effort.

Finally, Terrell decided to change schools. After talking with his mother and brothers — four of whom had also changed schools before — he transferred to Abraham Lincoln Preparatory High School in the middle of his sophomore year. Lincoln had only about eight hundred students, and although it lacked many of the facilities of Morse, Terrell didn't feel quite so lost.

The transfer gave him a chance to make a fresh start. Several teachers sensed his potential and took a special interest in him. He started going to class every day and began paying attention. His schoolwork immediately improved, and he discovered that he actually enjoyed his classes, particularly math.

His attitude toward school and everything else began to change. He came out of his shell and joined the track team. He discovered that he still had some of his old speed, and in the spring of 1988, he became a valuable member of the squad, running the quarter mile and throwing the discus.

One day he ran into his old Pop Warner coach, Frank White. They started talking and White told him, "You need to go back to playing football." Terrell agreed. That fall, he went out for the team.

Although it was a small school, Lincoln High had a strong football tradition. The great running back Marcus Allen had set all sorts of records at Lincoln before graduating in 1978. He later won the Heisman Trophy as the nation's best collegiate player at the University of Southern California, and then went on to a great career in the NFL with the Oakland Raiders and Kansas City Chiefs. A huge portrait of Allen hung on a wall in the school. Nearly every season a dozen or more players from Lincoln earned scholarships to play college football.

But Terrell Davis wasn't thinking about playing college football, much less playing in the NFL. He was already a junior and getting a late start to his high school career. Most of his teammates had been playing football since they were freshmen. Although he knew he was way behind, he just wanted to be part of the team.

At the start of practice, Davis told head coach Vic Player that he was a running back. Player took note of Terrell's speed and size — he had grown to nearly six feet tall and weighed 195 pounds — and agreed.

But despite his physical attributes and his years of playing Pop Warner ball, Terrell really didn't know how to play football. The plays the Lincoln Hornets used were much more complicated than those in the Pop Warner league. In Pop Warner, all Terrell used to do was take the ball and run on almost every play. Now he had to learn to block, run pass patterns, and do everything else a running back does when he isn't running the football.

Although he worked hard in practice every day

and loved putting on the green-and-white Lincoln uniform, he was stuck on the fourth string, behind three more-experienced backs. In the early part of the season, he never got a chance to play in a game.

One of Terrell's teammates, a defensive lineman named James Tufulu, was impressed in practice by how hard Terrell could hit and block. He knew Terrell was frustrated by not playing, so he told Terrell to ask to play defense.

At first, Terrell scoffed at the notion. He still envisioned himself as "Boss Hogg," a star running back. But he wanted to play so badly that he finally took his friend's advice and volunteered to play defense.

The Lincoln coaching staff agreed to let him try and in practice installed him at nose guard on the defensive line. The nose guard plays in the middle of the line, right over the opposing center. His job is to gum up the middle and occupy as many offensive linemen as possible, freeing the linebackers and other defensive linemen to make tackles.

The very next week, Terrell got his first chance to play in a game. Early in the contest, when the other team lined up to try a field goal, Coach Player sent Terrell into the game to play nose guard.

The responsibilities of the defensive linemen are different during a field-goal attempt than during a regular play from scrimmage. Everybody is supposed to try to bust through the line and block the kick.

Terrell lined up and looked at the ball out of the corner of his eye. As soon as he saw the center start to snap the ball, he fired toward the gap between the guard and center. He shot through the hole before either player could effectively block him. Then he jumped into the air toward the placeholder.

Thwump! The kicker met the ball with his foot.

Thwack! The football traveled about six feet before smacking hard into Terrell's upraised arm and bouncing backward. In his very first play, Terrell had blocked the kick!

His quickness immediately impressed his coaches, and the next time the defense took the field, they sent Terrell back in at nose guard. For the rest of the game he gave the opposition fits. He was just too fast and strong. He did more than just occupy blockers. He knifed in for tackles behind the line of scrimmage and sacked the quarterback almost at will. Coach Player later said that trying to block Terrell "was like trying to block a greased pig."

Davis loved it. After standing on the sidelines watching others play, now he was in the middle of the action. For the rest of the year, he was the Hornets' starting nose guard.

After football season, he rejoined the track team. After practicing hard all fall, he noticed he was faster and stronger than the year before. He set school records in the quarter-mile run and discus throw.

But he couldn't forget about how it had been running the football and being "Boss Hogg." When football practice resumed late the following summer, Davis asked his coaches if he could return to running back. He figured his senior year would be his last playing football and he wanted to run the ball again just like he had in the Pop Warner league.

There was only one problem: Despite the graduation of several players, Terrell was still only the third-best running back on the team. In Lincoln's usual offense, they used only two running backs at a time. But that didn't stop Terrell. He played so well in practice that Coach Player decided to change the team's offensive scheme to take advantage of his ability. He switched from the I-formation, which features two running backs lined up one behind the other, to a three-back formation, with two halfbacks and a fullback. Terrell Davis became the fullback.

But there was a catch. Terrell had become such a good nose guard that the coaches wanted him to play both offense and defense. Terrell knew it would be fatiguing playing almost every down, but he didn't complain. In fact, he loved it.

Much of the time, the fullback's primary responsibility is to block for one of the halfbacks. After spending a year on defense hitting people, Terrell had become a devastating blocker.

Privately, the coaches actually believed that Terrell was as good at running the ball as Lincoln's two halfbacks. But he was such a good blocker, he was more valuable to the team playing fullback. At first, he was usually the third option to run the ball. Then, as the season progressed, the coaches started calling running plays for him more often. And the more they put the ball into his hands, the better he ran, barreling right over people just as he had in Pop Warner football. He also showed surprising quickness and a stunning ability to cut back against the grain of the defense.

Terrell Davis was quickly becoming a one-man team, filling in wherever he was needed. He occasionally played tight end and also started kicking off for the team, often beating his teammates downfield and tackling the runner. With all this in addition to his standout performance at nose guard, people started noticing Terrell Davis. It was hard not to. He was all over the field.

Terrell helped lead Lincoln to a great season. They finished 12–2 and even got to play for the division championship at San Diego's Jack Murphy Stadium, where the NFL's Chargers played. Although they lost the game, it was one of the most successful seasons in Lincoln history.

Despite missing several games late in the year with a separated shoulder, Terrell still gained more than seven hundred yards rushing. He even made the all-league team. By the end of the season, a number of college football programs expressed interest in him.

In college athletics, schools are divided into three divisions. Division One is the best. Schools in Division One often offer athletes full scholarships, paying room, board, and tuition. At Division Two and Three schools, the competition isn't as good and schools aren't allowed to offer full scholarships.

A number of Division Two and Division Three colleges contacted Terrell and tried to convince him to attend their schools. He was flattered but couldn't consider their offers. Without a full scholarship, he couldn't go to college. His mother simply didn't have the money.

Only two Division One colleges expressed interest in Terrell, Utah State and Long Beach State University, in California. Both schools asked Terrell to visit.

When he arrived at Utah State in Logan, Utah, he was impressed by the facilities and the beautiful campus. But he was also looking forward to having some fun in college. He met with several players and asked them about going out at night. They just started laughing. They explained to Terrell that Logan was a small town and that Utah was a very conservative place. There wasn't any nightlife in Logan, Utah.

So Terrell visited Long Beach State in Long Beach, California, just south of Los Angeles and only a few hundred miles from San Diego. He was already familiar with the school. His older brother Reggie played running back at Long Beach State.

In fact, it was Reggie who had alerted the coaching staff at Long Beach about Terrell, telling them there was another player out of Lincoln High who could help them. The coaches didn't know Reggie and Terrell were brothers. That's because Reggie's last name was Webb. Terrell and Reggie were only half brothers. Reggie had been born while Joe Davis was in prison and their mother was in a relationship with another man.

Terrell loved his visit to Long Beach State. The school was right on the ocean and there was a lot more to do in the area than in Utah. And although Long Beach didn't have a strong football tradition, that seemed about ready to change. Their coach, George Allen, was a legend.

Allen had been a successful coach in professional football for the Los Angeles Rams and Washington Redskins, even leading the Redskins to the Super Bowl. He had retired only to discover he missed coaching. So he decided to coach college football. After coaching professionals for so many years, he loved teaching younger men how to play the game.

Allen met with Terrell and the two liked each other from the start. Allen told Terrell he saw his future as a running back and offered him a full scholarship. Terrell immediately accepted.

"Boss Hogg" was going to college.

Chapter Three:
1990–1992

A Chance in College

Terrell Davis began attending Long Beach State in the fall of 1990. From the first moment he stepped on the campus, he was in love.

He enjoyed every minute with Coach Allen, who had everyone's respect. Allen didn't yell at players or make them feel stupid. Instead, he tried to explain the game and teach them specific techniques. Terrell felt as if he was studying the game under an old master. And he was.

He loved everything else about college, too, even going to class and studying. He had no illusions about playing football for a living. A pro football career was almost impossible to imagine. Although Long Beach State was a Division One school, the team competed in a weak conference. Long Beach State was a long way from the National Football

League. Only a few former Long Beach players had ever played in the NFL.

Davis knew that football was only part of the reason he was in college. His education was more important. He enjoyed mathematics and majored in consumer economics. Eventually, he hoped to become an accountant.

But that didn't mean he didn't want to have fun, too. He went to parties, met girls, and hung out with people whose backgrounds were far different from his. He liked living on his own for the first time in his life.

After sizing up Terrell's abilities, Allen and the Long Beach coaching staff decided to have him "redshirt" his freshman year. That meant that while he was allowed to practice with the team, he wasn't allowed to play in any games.

Redshirting is a common practice in collegiate football. Many freshmen aren't prepared, physically, socially, or academically, to step in and play in their first season. By redshirting for a year, a player still retains his eligibility to play four full seasons of college football but has a year to mature and adjust to college life. Besides, Long Beach had plenty of running backs, including his older brother Reggie Webb, so Terrell wouldn't have had much of a chance to play that year anyway. Several players were scheduled to graduate that year, and Davis would receive a better opportunity to play in the 1991 season. It made a lot of sense for him to red-shirt. Davis didn't mind. He knew that with his late start, he had a lot to learn about football.

He still got to practice and spent much of the fall performing on the scout team. Each week in practice, college scout teams imitate the opposition, running the same plays, so the regular team will be familiar with their formations and strategy on Saturday. It was a good opportunity for Terrell to learn, and by playing against the first string every week, he improved rapidly.

He quickly became one of Allen's favorite players. Davis was quiet and humble, and didn't act like a hot dog on the field. He just did his job as best as he could.

By the end of the season, the first string could barely stop him. Because of the strong, smooth way he ran the football, Allen started calling him "Secretariat," after a world-famous Thoroughbred racehorse. Every time Terrell heard Allen yell, "There goes Secretariat!" he had to suppress a smile.

Though football was going well, Davis didn't complete his freshman year without his share of problems. To get around campus, he had a car, an old Chevy Impala. One night a friend told him he'd seen a car with some expensive spoke rims that would look great on Davis's car. When he suggested they steal them, Davis, without thinking of the consequences, simply responded, "Cool."

Neither Davis nor his buddy was an experienced thief. They didn't even bring a jack to lift the car off the ground. Instead, they spent hours trying to hoist the car by hand onto crates and blocks of wood so they could remove the rims.

Needless to say, they were eventually spotted by passersby. Someone called the police. As the police watched incredulously, the two young men, oblivious of their presence, grappled with the car and put the rims on Davis's Impala. As soon as they tried to make their getaway, the police moved in. The two were caught before they'd driven fifty feet.

Davis spent four days in jail, charged with grand theft, before his mother could secure his release.

Then she had to hire a lawyer to plead his case before a judge.

Davis was incredibly embarrassed by the experience. He had a clean record and knew he'd made a foolish mistake. But he felt even worse knowing he'd let his mother down. Fortunately, the judge took his background into account, lowered the charge to a misdemeanor, and gave him probation. After that, Davis promised himself he'd never get in trouble with the law again, and to this day he has kept that promise. He learned his lesson.

Long Beach finished the season with a 6–5 record. Davis could hardly wait for the 1991 season to begin. He looked forward to playing for real for a change.

But before the 1991 season, Coach Allen, who was seventy-two years old, became sick with pneumonia and died. Willie Brown, one of Allen's assistants, who had played professionally for the Oakland Raiders and Denver Broncos, was hired as his replacement.

Brown didn't make many changes. Terrell moved from the practice squad to the regular team. But he didn't make the first string. Reggie Webb, in his senior season, started at running back. Davis began the season as a backup.

At first, Davis played sparingly. But as the season progressed, Long Beach struggled. As they did, Coach Brown began taking a long look at younger players on the team, including Davis.

Terrell ended up starting four games and finished second in rushing to Reggie Webb, gaining 262 yards on 55 carries, with two touchdowns. He also caught four passes for 92 yards, including a 78-yard touchdown reception against the University of Nevada, Las Vegas. In the end, though, Long Beach finished the season a disappointing 2–9.

Still, Davis looked forward to the upcoming season. He seemed certain to take over as starting tailback, and he was confident that he would finally be able to demonstrate his talent and lead his team to a winning season.

But a short time after the end of the season, Davis was relaxing in his dorm room when a friend rushed in.

"Did you hear the news?" he asked Davis breathlessly.

"What news?" said Davis.

"They just dropped the football program!" responded his friend.

Davis couldn't believe it. Just a few years before, Long Beach had hired George Allen to build the program up. But after Allen's death, the school reconsidered. Football was an expensive sport, and Long Beach drew only a few thousand fans to each game. By dropping the program, they could save money and spend their limited resources on other sports.

Davis was stunned. Just as he was getting comfortable in his new life as a college student, the unthinkable had happened. All of a sudden, he had to either give up football or find another place to play. After weighing all the factors, Terrell decided to change schools.

Normally, when a player transfers from one school to another, he must sit out a year before becoming eligible to play again. But since Long Beach was dropping the program, members of the team could transfer and be eligible to play immediately.

This made many of the Long Beach players attractive to other schools. Not only were they already experienced, another school wouldn't have to use a full four-year scholarship on them.

Most of the players took matters into their own hands and put together videotapes of their play to send around to colleges. But Davis was lucky. College scouts had noted his fine play the previous year and now *they* sought *him* out.

He received a few feelers from schools on the West Coast before getting a message asking him to call a recruiter for the University of Georgia. Davis didn't know much about Georgia, but he called back. The school invited him to visit.

The football program at the University of Georgia was radically different from that of Long Beach State. At Long Beach, the program had been run on a shoestring budget. But at Georgia, football was huge.

The university had just celebrated its one hundredth season of collegiate football. Glenn "Pop" Warner, the man after whom the Pop Warner football program was named, had once been the Georgia Bulldogs' coach.

The program was very successful. The team had won five national championships and had played in the greatest variety of postseason bowl games of any school in the country. Dozens of Georgia players had gone on to careers in professional football, including running back and Heisman Trophy winner Herschel Walker.

The team played in huge, historic Sanford Stadium before tens of thousands of fans and competed in the Southeastern Conference (SEC), one of the toughest leagues in the country. Virtually every game was broadcast on television.

Davis was blown away by his visit. The campus, in Athens, Georgia, was beautiful. And the facilities for football were fabulous. The carpeted locker room was huge and the team had its own weight-training facility. During his visit they presented Davis with equipment — cleats and helmets and T-shirts — and an escort even led him to a locker where a jersey was hanging with his name on the back. Davis was ready to play right that instant. He immediately accepted Georgia's scholarship offer and made plans to transfer.

In retrospect, he might have made a mistake. He was so impressed with the facilities that he didn't realize Georgia already had a star running back, Garrison Hearst, who still had eligibility remaining. Nor did he really get to know Georgia coach Ray Goff.

But at that moment, he didn't care. He had found a place to play. "Boss Hogg" was gonna be a Bulldog.

Chapter Four:
1992–1994

The Bulldog

Davis knew he had a lot to learn about the Georgia program and wanted to get off to a quick start. He transferred as soon as he could so he would be able to participate in spring practice. He thought he had been given a golden opportunity and was determined to make the most of it. Success or failure would depend solely on his actions.

That point had been driven home in the most dramatic and tragic fashion just a few weeks earlier. His older brother Bobby had been in and out of trouble since their father's death. That spring he had tried to rob a pregnant woman. When she resisted, he shot her. Although she survived, the baby she was carrying died. He eventually served five years in prison for his crime.

Davis knew only too well how quickly and easily

bad decisions could ruin a person's life. He was determined to escape the cycle of crime and violence that had devastated his family. He wanted to make more of himself.

Although he didn't have a prayer of beating out Garrison Hearst, he impressed Coach Goff during practice, scored a touchdown during the annual spring game, and was listed as the third-string "scatback," Georgia's name for the featured running back in their offense.

He worked out all summer long. When football practice started again in August, he concentrated on learning the subtleties of the Georgia offense. His hard work paid off. At the beginning of the season, he moved up to be Hearst's backup.

But once the 1992 regular season started, he hardly played, at least not when it mattered. Georgia was touting the talented Hearst as a Heisman Trophy candidate, and he played all or most of every game, usually leaving the lineup only when the Bulldogs were far ahead. Davis only got to play late in the game or for a play or two now and then when Hearst had to take a breather.

But despite his limited playing time, when Davis

did get the ball, he made an impression. He finished the season as the team's number two rusher, with 388 yards and a team-leading 7.3-yard average per carry. He scored three touchdowns, including one dash of 61 yards. The team finished the season with a 10–2 record, including a 21–14 win over powerful Ohio State in the Citrus Bowl.

After the season, Hearst went on to the NFL, where he was the number one draft pick of the Arizona Cardinals. At spring practice in 1993, Davis took over as the starting scatback.

He was thrilled. Playing for a high-profile, top-notch program at Georgia, he knew that if he did well he might attract the attention of pro scouts. Although he'd never given the idea of playing professional football a serious thought before, for the first time, he began to dream about playing in the NFL.

That dream appeared to move closer to reality during the 1993 season, at least at the beginning. Davis exploded out of the gate with a series of strong performances, including a 131-yard showing against the University of Tennessee, and 171 yards versus the University of Arkansas. The Bulldog running game wasn't missing a beat without Hearst.

Unfortunately, that didn't result in victories. Georgia's defense was terrible, and despite all the yards Davis gained, the Bulldogs lost to both Tennessee and Arkansas. The team was struggling. Coach Goff suddenly found himself under pressure from the press and some alumni. So he decided to change tactics. Quarterback Eric Zeier had put together two strong performances, and Goff decided to pass the ball more.

As a result, Davis's playing time suffered. By the end of the season, although he led the team with 824 yards rushing, he was a part-time player again. Georgia finished the season a disappointing 5–6.

Davis was confused. Coach Goff had never bothered explaining his change of strategy, and Davis wondered if Goff had lost confidence in his ability. With only one year of college remaining, Davis was determined to make his final season at Georgia something special.

Then Davis's world was turned upside down.

In high school, his best friend, Jamaul Pennington, had been one of the many people taken in by Davis's mother. He lived with the family, and the two friends had become as close as brothers.

That summer, while Davis remained in Georgia working out for his upcoming senior season, he received some terrible news. On July 27, Jamaul was shot in a disturbance police described as "gang-related." He was dropped off at a hospital and died later that evening.

Davis was devastated by the news. He returned to San Diego for his friend's funeral and remained there for several weeks mourning Pennington's death. Then Goff called him at home and pushed him to return.

Davis thought the coach was insensitive, but he reluctantly returned. Soon after, however, he pulled the hamstring muscle in his right leg.

The hamstring is the big muscle in the back of the upper leg. It can be notoriously hard to heal, and if not healed completely, is prone to re-injury.

Goff didn't believe Davis was hurt very badly and pressured him to keep practicing. He did, but the leg kept bothering him.

Davis limped through the season opener, a 24–21 win over South Carolina, but early in a 41–23 loss to Tennessee the following week, he injured the hamstring even worse than before.

Davis blamed Goff, but Goff refused to believe he was seriously injured. The relationship between the player and coach deteriorated badly.

Over the next several weeks, Davis hardly played as Goff turned more and more to the passing game. But without a running game to keep the defense honest, opponents were able to put all their efforts into stopping the passing game. The Bulldogs struggled as they had the previous season.

With only two games remaining in his collegiate career, Davis had reached the breaking point. His chances of playing in the NFL seemed remote. Since he'd hardly played all year long, he knew that no pro football team was likely to give him a chance.

So the week before the Auburn game, healthy at last, he decided to go for broke. He had the best practice week of his career, shredding the scout team with a series of long runs and playing with reckless abandon. Then, at a team meeting the night before the game, he stood up before the whole team and with uncharacteristic brashness announced, "If you give me the ball, I'll get a hundred yards."

The team took him up on his challenge the next day, and Davis didn't disappoint them. He rumbled for 113 yards against the tough Auburn defense. The Bulldogs managed to tie their favored opponents, 13–13.

One week later, in his final collegiate game, Davis did it again. This time he ran for 125 yards and scored two touchdowns against Georgia's archrival, Georgia Tech. The victory enabled Georgia to finish the season above .500, with a record of 6–4–1.

Although he was pleased to end his college career on a high note, Davis worried that it was too little, too late. He ended the season with only 445 rushing yards, barely half his total from the year before. He hoped that would be enough to attract the attention of an NFL team but worried he'd be overlooked in the upcoming draft.

Then, just a few weeks after the end of the season, he got a lucky break. The annual Blue-Gray Game, named for the colors of the uniforms worn during the Civil War, is an all-star contest that features collegiate players from the South playing against their counterparts from the North. Only the best players in the country are asked to play in the Christmas Day exhibition. When a better-known running back withdrew from the game due to an injury, Davis was asked to replace him on the roster.

He was excited to be on the team. He would have at least one more chance to impress the pro scouts.

He practiced well with the team and during the game got to play more than several other running backs. He ripped off a number of impressive runs and even threw a touchdown pass on a halfback-option play. He hoped the NFL scouts had been paying attention.

They had. Terrell received an invitation to attend the NFL combine held in Indianapolis in February. He still had a shot at playing professional football.

The combine is like a big tryout camp. Every NFL team sends virtually its entire coaching staff to the combine. Each of the several hundred players invited to attend is given a physical exam and a battery of psychological and intelligence tests, then is put through a thorough series of workouts so he can be evaluated under a controlled set of conditions. Players run timed races between and around cones, called the "shuttle," do the broad jump, lift weights, and have their vertical leaps measured. Some players with average collegiate careers have become first-round draft picks based solely on their performances at the combine. On the other hand, some stars discover that their stock has dropped dramatically after a poor performance.

Perhaps the most important test at the combine, particularly for a running back, is the forty-yard dash. A player's time in the forty-yard dash is the major yardstick by which many scouts and coaches compare players. Even after studying hours of film of a player, they consider the forty-yard-dash time to be the final word on a player's speed and quickness.

Others consider the race to be an artificial test. Players run from a standing start without wearing football equipment. The sprint doesn't measure a back's ability to cut, find a hole in the line, run while holding a football, or avoid pursuit.

For players at the speed positions on a football field — defensive back, wide receiver, and running back — a time of 4.5 seconds or less is almost mandatory. Even linemen weighing three hundred pounds or more are expected to run in five seconds or less.

Davis found the combine exhausting. The forty-yard dash was the last test.

Davis lined up and waited for the signal to start running. When he heard the whistle, he took off and ran as fast as he could.

He crossed the finish line and immediately turned back to learn his time. The combine official shouted out, "Four point seven!"

Four point seven? Davis was crushed. The time was slow for a running back. His chances of making the NFL seemed to evaporate.

But NFL teams keep evaluating players right up until the day of the draft in April. They tour the major colleges in the spring and work out prospective players one last time, both to make sure their earlier evaluations are correct and to ensure that no talented player has somehow fallen through the cracks.

Knowing this, Davis decided he had to make some changes. In his final opportunity to impress the pro scouts, he wanted to be in the best shape of his career. He didn't want to go through the rest of his life wondering if he had blown his chance by not working hard enough.

To that end, he hired a husband-and-wife team of personal trainers. For several weeks, they took over his life, putting him on a special diet, giving him all sorts of nutritional supplements, and pushing him through a series of grueling workouts.

His teammates at Georgia laughed at all the work Davis was doing. They thought his chances of making the NFL were negligible and that he was wasting his time. But they couldn't measure his determination. Over the course of several weeks he got into the best possible physical condition.

It paid off. At the campus workouts he stunned the scouts by shaving three-tenths of a second off his time in the forty-yard dash, from 4.7 to 4.4. All of a sudden, several teams began to take another look at Terrell Davis. That was the kind of speed the NFL was looking for.

Now, Davis hoped that on draft day someone would remember his name.

Chapter Five:
1995

Sixth-Round Starter

In the weeks before the draft, several teams began courting Terrell. It still wasn't certain he'd be one of the players drafted in the seven-round NFL draft, but he was now reasonably confident that some team would sign him as a free agent. To get on his good side, teams interested in Davis, like the Green Bay Packers, Tampa Bay Buccaneers, and Cleveland Browns, spoke with him personally and gave him all sorts of equipment. They hoped that if he slipped through the draft, he would decide to accept their free-agent offer.

As draft day approached, Davis was full of anticipation — and a little worried. He hoped to be drafted, but when he looked over some draft projections put together by the media, he became alarmed.

Most projections had Davis far down on the list of prospects, behind twenty or thirty other running backs. Some came right out and said he had absolutely no chance of making it in the NFL, much less being drafted. One so-called draft guru said that it would be foolish for any team even to sign him as a free agent.

Davis tried not to let his expectations get too high before the draft. He knew that a career in the NFL was still a longshot.

The draft is held over a two-day period in April and is broadcast live on ESPN. On the first day of the draft, Davis was low-key. He knew he had little chance of hearing his name in the first three rounds and didn't even bother watching the draft on television. That night, he went to a big party, and he slept until noon the next day. When he awoke, he went to a friend's house to watch the remainder of the draft.

The draft was already well into the fourth round and Davis still hadn't been picked. As each pick was announced, his hopes grew dimmer. At the end of the fifth round, he still hadn't been selected. The ESPN broadcast ended. The remainder of the draft was broadcast only on ESPN2, which his friend didn't have.

Davis was resigned to being a free agent. Disappointed but trying to hide it, he went to a barbecue while a representative of his agent went to a sports bar to watch the rest of the draft.

Meanwhile, the coaching staffs and scouts of every NFL team huddled together trying to decide whom to choose next, crossing off names with each pick, working on trades, and trying to decide how best to use their draft choices.

Because of trades and free-agent signings, the Denver Broncos didn't even have a draft pick in the first three rounds. All their picks were in the fourth round or later. Coach Mike Shanahan wanted to use those picks to help shore up Denver's offensive and defensive lines.

But offensive coordinator Gary Kubiak disagreed. He thought the team needed a running back. He knew the premier running backs would all be gone by the fourth round, so he put together a list of "sleepers," backs with a lot of potential who still might be available in the later rounds. One of the names on his list was Terrell Davis. He had scouted Davis in the Blue-Gray Game and been impressed.

He wasn't the only one on the Bronco staff who felt that way. Earlier that year a scout had written a so-so report on Davis but then added "there might be more here than what I saw."

The reports impressed Shanahan. After choosing a number of linemen, when it came time for the Broncos' second pick in the sixth round, they chose Davis.

Moments after they made their pick, Davis got a phone call. He was still in the midst of the barbecue.

It was his agent's partner. "Terrell!" he shouted breathlessly into the phone. "The Denver Broncos picked you in the sixth round."

Incredulous, Davis repeated those words to everyone at the barbecue. As the words sunk in, people surrounded him, clapping him on the back and offering him congratulations.

But Davis didn't know what to think. "Denver?" he kept asking himself. "I was picked by *Denver?*"

In the weeks and months before the draft, he hadn't heard a single word from the Denver Broncos. He knew little about the team, apart from the fact that the great John Elway was Denver's quarterback, and that it was very cold in the winter in Denver. They'd drafted him, but he wasn't sure they really wanted him.

His mother sensed his confusion and tried to cheer him up. "You should be happy," she told him.

Davis disagreed. Being drafted was only one small step toward what he really wanted, which was to play in the NFL.

"No, Mom," he told her, "the day I'll be happy is when I'm the starting running back."

The more Davis learned about the Denver Broncos, the less likely it seemed that he'd reach that day with them. The Broncos were a veteran team with a new coach, Mike Shanahan, about whom Davis knew nothing. For years, the Broncos had won and lost behind the strong right arm of Elway. They were primarily a passing team. The running game was an afterthought.

He also learned that he was the only rookie running back the team had selected. If they were planning to run the football more, they probably would have selected a running back earlier in the draft. Besides, they already had five veteran halfbacks on the roster and would probably keep only two or three. Of all the backs in the draft, Davis had been the twenty-first picked, the 196th player selected over-all. His chances of making the team appeared to be almost nonexistent. Right before training camp be-gan, one member of the press described his chances of making the team as not "slim and none," but "none and none."

But at the same time, Denver's lack of a running game gave Davis a unique opportunity. No running back on the team was a lock to make the squad. Even the veterans would have to play their way onto the final roster.

Davis was nervous when he arrived at training camp at the University of Northern Colorado in Greeley, Colorado, in July of 1995. Pro football training camps are tough, and Davis had heard hor-ror stories about players simply giving up and sneak-ing away in the middle of the night. Terrell knew he'd never do that — he'd worked far too hard to make it to this point — but still, he was more than a little scared.

When he arrived and tried to check in to camp, he received confirmation of just how remote his chances of making the team were. He was stopped by a security guard. Davis had forgotten the ID the Broncos had sent him, and at first the guard didn't believe he was a member of the team. Terrell Davis was about as unknown as any rookie to ever try to make an NFL team.

The first few days of camp Davis kept his mouth shut, worked hard, and watched veteran players to see how they behaved. He knew it wouldn't do him any good if he came to camp and started acting like he was a big shot.

But he quickly learned that his prospects weren't quite as grim as he had feared. He heard members of the media and even some veteran players complain that the Broncos' big problem was their lack of a running game. Without it, the opposition knew they were going to pass most of the time, which made the Broncos easy to defend.

Over the first few weeks of camp, he got little chance to prove himself. Davis and other low draft picks and free agents were ignored by almost everyone. They joked with one another that they were "camp meat," brought in to give the regulars someone to practice against. Davis was the sixth-string halfback on a team with only six halfbacks. It hadn't even been that bad at Lincoln High!

Still, Davis was thrilled as he pulled on the Bronco uniform for the Broncos' first exhibition game, versus San Francisco at Denver's Mile High Stadium on July 29. But as the game progressed, he got more and more depressed. He was on the field for only one play, a dive up the middle, and he was stopped for no gain.

Afterward, however, he received his first words of encouragement when assistant coach and offensive coordinator Gary Kubiak apologized for not playing him more. He promised he'd get more playing time the next game. That made Davis feel a little better. At least he knew he'd still be on the team until then!

The Broncos played their next exhibition against the 49ers again, in Tokyo. The team traveled to Japan several days ahead of time to practice.

Davis had a terrible week. No matter what he did, one of the Bronco coaches was on his back, screaming at him to try harder. He felt that he was already working as hard as possible. The constant criticism frustrated him.

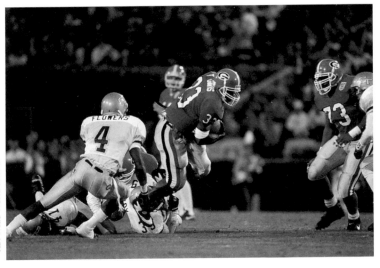

Georgia running back Terrell Davis moves the ball downfield before being tackled by a player from archrival Georgia Tech. Georgia won hands down, 48–10.

Terrell Davis has the moves to fend off the attack! The Broncos defeated the Chiefs in this AFC playoff game in 1998.

Touchdown! Terrell Davis scores the first points for the Broncos in Super Bowl XXXII on January 25, 1998.

The onset of a devastating migraine headache temporarily sidelines Terrell Davis during Super Bowl XXXII.

After scoring the winning touchdown in Super Bowl XXXII, Terrell Davis gives the Broncos' trademark military salute.

Victory celebration, Super Bowl XXXII! Terrell Davis holds aloft the Lombardi Trophy following the Broncos' defeat of the Packers, 31–24.

Super Bowl XXXII MVP Terrell Davis.

A man in motion, Terrell Davis takes off for a 20-yard touchdown run.

With the thrills come some spills. . . . Terrell Davis is tripped up by a Seattle Seahawk.

Two-time Super Bowl champs Terrell Davis and quarterback John Elway try on their caps following their Super Bowl XXXIII victory on January 31, 1999.

Terrell Davis's Career Stats

Regular Season Record

		Rushing				Receiving			
Year	Team	Carries	Yards	Average	TD	Catches	Yards	Average	TD
1995	Denver	237	1,117	4.7	7	49	367	7.5	1
1996	Denver	345	1,538	4.5	13	36	310	8.6	2
1997	Denver	369	1,750	4.7	15	42	287	6.8	0
1998	Denver	392	2,008	5.1	21	25	217	8.7	2
Career Totals		1343	6,413	4.8	56	152	1,181	7.8	5

Postseason Record

		Rushing				Receiving			
Year	Team	Carries	Yards	Average	TD	Catches	Yards	Average	TD
1996	Denver	14	91	6.5	1	7	24	3.4	1
1997	Denver	112	581	5.2	8	8	38	4.8	0
1998	Denver	78	468	6.0	3	4	69	17.3	3
Career Totals		204	1,140	5.6	12	19	131	6.9	4

Terrell Davis's Career Highlights

1995:

Led team in rushing

Voted by Broncos as team's Offensive MVP

Second in voting for NFL Offensive Rookie of the Year

Selected by *Football Digest* as Rookie of the Year

Voted to All-Rookie teams by *Pro Football Weekly* and *Football News*

Selected as Pro Bowl alternate

1996:

First in rushing in AFC, second in NFL

Named AFC Player of the Month (September)

Set new single-season Bronco records for rushing, carries, and touchdowns

Selected for the Pro Bowl

1997:

(Regular Season)

First in rushing in AFC, second in NFL

Named AFC Player of the Month (September)

Selected for the Pro Bowl

(Postseason)

Super Bowl XXXII MVP

With three touchdowns, tied Super Bowl record for most points
  scored and most touchdowns scored

1998:

(Regular Season)

Named NFL MVP

Named NFL Offensive Player of the Year

Named AFC Player of the Month twice (September and October)

Named AFC Player of the Week four times

Won NFL rushing title

(Postseason)

Set NFL rushing record (2,476 yards, regular and postseason totals
  combined)

Set NFL records for postseason rushing averages (142.5 yards per
  game, 5.6 yards per attempt)

Set NFL record for most consecutive 100-yard rushing games in
  postseason (7)

One evening at the team hotel, Davis decided he'd had enough. He decided to quit.

He picked up the telephone and tried to arrange a flight back to the United States. But he didn't speak Japanese and the operator didn't speak English very well. He couldn't get through to an airline, so he decided to give himself just a few more days.

That may have been the most important decision Davis made since deciding to play football again in high school. Because during the game, Kubiak made good on his promise.

Davis got into the game in the second half. He was handed the football and made a nice gain. Then he got the ball again and ripped off another five yards. Although he was alternating with several other Bronco running backs, only Davis was gaining any yardage. He even scored a touchdown.

But what really got everyone's attention was his special-teams play. Play on special teams — kick-offs, punts, and field-goal and extra-point attempts — is important in the NFL. Players are supposed to give everything they have. Few regular players are asked to play on specials because it's so dangerous. But playing on special teams is a great way for a rookie to make a name for himself. Players some-times make the team based solely upon their special-teams performance.

Midway through the third quarter, Davis went in when the Broncos kicked off to San Francisco. It was the first time he had played on a kickoff team since attending Long Beach State.

The Bronco kicker booted the ball high and deep to the San Francisco return man, Tyronne Drake-ford. Davis took off with the kick and streaked downfield, slipping past a blocker on his way. He saw Drakeford catch the ball near the goal line and head upfield.

Davis took dead aim on the ball carrier. He felt like he was a Lincoln High nose guard moving in to make a sack again. He slipped past another blocker and rocketed toward Drakeford. *Wham!* With the power of a locomotive, he stopped Drakeford in his tracks and drove him back several yards.

It was a great play, and Davis knew it. He jumped high in celebration, punching the air with his fist and screaming.

When he got back to the sidelines, veterans who had otherwise almost ignored him gave him high-fives and words of encouragement. Even John Elway said, "Way to go!" Lineman Michael Dean Perry was even more supportive. "On that hit, you just made the team," he said, smiling.

Davis finished the game with 46 yards on 11 carries, twice the yardage of any other Bronco halfback, plus a touchdown, helping the Broncos to a 24–10 win. After the game, Coach Shanahan approached him and said, "T.D., good job."

His play even got the attention of the press back in Colorado. When the team returned to camp, the reporters speculated that he just might make the team and sought him out for the first time. "I'm trying to keep everything in perspective," he told them. "I have to improve in every phase [of the game]. But I'm happy where I am right now."

Later that week, as the team studied video of the exhibition game, Shanahan stopped and showed the replay of Davis's tackle on the kickoff over and over. "This is the way you play the game," he told the squad. "This is how it is done."

The coaches started giving Davis more of their attention. In the next exhibition, against Carolina, he ran the ball only once for six yards, but caught four passes for 47 yards and returned four kickoffs for 100 yards.

The following week in practice Davis vaulted up the chart to second string behind Glyn Milburn. In an exhibition game against the Dallas Cowboys, he rumbled for an impressive 73 yards on ten carries. His performance earned him a chance to run behind the first-string offensive line in the final exhibition game, against Jacksonville, a week later. Again he responded to the challenge, gaining 46 yards on seven attempts. Davis was now convinced he had made the team.

But the club still had a few players to cut. Usually when a player is cut, an assistant or some other official comes up to him and asks him to go see the coach. Most rookies and fringe players spend much of training camp looking over their shoulders in fear of being approached and hearing those words.

One day later that week, the team was preparing for its season opener against the Buffalo Bills. The Broncos' assistant personnel director walked up to Davis and said, "Coach wants to see you."

Davis looked up and felt a large lump form in his

throat. Coach Shanahan had never asked to see him before. Davis was petrified.

He went to Coach's office, took a deep breath, and knocked on the door. Shanahan asked him in and told him to take a seat. Davis feared the worst.

Shanahan paused for a moment and the tension mounted. Finally, his face expressionless, the coach spoke. "You're our starting running back," he said.

Davis couldn't suppress a huge smile of relief. He was happier than he had ever been in his life.

Chapter Six:
1995

Rookie Surprise

The first thing the new starting running back of the Denver Broncos did was buy a brand-new car. Then he had to find an apartment in Denver and prepare to live on his own in the real world for the first time.

He still couldn't believe his good fortune. He almost had to pinch himself in practice when, working out with the entire first team for the first time, he looked up and saw John Elway calling the plays in the huddle. Elway had been a star for years, and Davis had watched him play on television. Now, unbelievable as it seemed, he was playing alongside Elway.

The Broncos opened the season against the Buffalo Bills. Although the Bills had stumbled to an uncharacteristic 7–9 record in 1994, they were still one of the best teams in the league. They were particularly noted for their tough defense, keyed by defensive end Bruce Smith and linebacker Cornelius Bennett. Both were among the hardest-hitting defensive players in the league.

On the Broncos' first possession, they moved quickly downfield. On third down and goal from the nine-yard line, Elway called for a short pass to Davis.

When the ball was snapped, Davis swung out the backfield toward the sideline and looked back for the ball. Elway's pass floated into his hands and he turned upfield. Only one player, cornerback Marlon Kemer, stood between him and the end zone. Davis should have just put down his head and driven the defender back. Instead, he made a rookie mistake — he tried to jump over him.

That probably would have worked in high school, and may have worked in college. But this was the NFL. Kemer wasn't fooled and hit Davis in midair, somersaulting him to the ground short of a touchdown.

In the third quarter, Elway threw another pass his way. Just as Terrell touched the ball, he was hit. The ball popped out of his hands and into those of a

Buffalo defender for an interception. So far, Davis was playing like the rookie he was.

Those two gaffs might have discouraged another player, but Davis was determined not to let his mistakes get him down. In the fourth quarter, with the Broncos ahead, 15–7, on five field goals by kicker Jason Elam, Denver drove to the Buffalo three-yard line. The Bronco coaching staff, showing confidence in their rookie running back, sent in a play calling for him to run the ball.

This time he didn't try to get cute. He put his head down and barreled into the end zone. Then he nonchalantly flipped the ball onto the ground as if he'd done it a hundred times before.

Davis's first touchdown as a professional secured a 22–7 win. Despite his two mistakes, he had rushed for a credible 70 yards. But he had to admit that his first real NFL game had been an eye-opener.

"I'm sore," he told the press after the game. "The game was much faster than I anticipated." But he wasn't intimidated. He knew he belonged.

He continued to play well, getting a little better each time out. The Broncos struggled, particularly on defense, but it was beginning to look as if they had finally found a running game. Davis was running for more yardage than any other rookie in the league, including the Chicago Bears' Rashaan Salaam, the 1994 Heisman Trophy winner.

The press was beginning to realize that Davis, and not Salaam, was the better rookie. Davis used Salaam for motivation, for the two young men had grown up in the same neighborhood and known each other since Pop Warner league.

Davis was surprising everyone. Not only was he faster than most observers thought, he was stronger, too. He was just as likely to run over a tackler as he was to run around them. He was a devastating blocker, was becoming a good receiver, and seemed to grow stronger as the game went on.

Davis also had an uncanny knack for dodging tacklers. He wasn't particularly flashy, doing 360s or reversing field, but with the defense in pursuit he seemed to know precisely when to cut the other way and leave the defender grabbing at the air.

On November 5, the Arizona Cardinals came to Mile High Stadium with a two-game winning streak.

Coach Buddy Ryan was known as a defensive specialist and the Cards had a reputation for playing tough.

To help open up the passing game, the Broncos decided to start the game by shoving the ball right down the Cardinals' throats. And they decided Terrell Davis was just the guy to do so.

Instead of using three wide receivers, they started the game with two tight ends and only two wide receivers, as if announcing their intention to run the ball. And from the first play of the game, that's what Denver did. They dared the Cardinals to stop Davis.

On his second carry of the game, Davis demonstrated the futility of trying to do that. He cracked through a hole, powered off-tackle, and shot into the secondary. Arizona safety Lorenzo Lynch moved up fast to attempt the tackle.

Davis saw him coming, faked hard one way, then cut the other. Lynch fell hard as he wrapped his arms around Davis's shadow. "I set him up with a move," Terrell would later say.

The running back rumbled 34 yards on the play

before being pulled down. A few plays later, Davis ran in for a touchdown from the five-yard line, capping a 60-yard performance on the opening drive.

Davis's play opened up the defense. For the rest of the game Elway picked the Cardinals apart with play-action passes. Davis picked up the tough yardage whenever it was needed. The Broncos won going away, 38–6. Terrell had his first 100-yard game as a pro, rushing for 135 yards, the most for a Denver running back at Mile High Stadium in more than twenty years.

After the game, quarterback John Elway, who had exceeded the 40,000-yard mark for career passing during the game, didn't want to talk about his own accomplishments. He wanted to talk about Davis.

"He made some unbelievable runs," Elway said. "His running opened up the game. He's amazing, to be a rookie and do what he's done. I haven't said it before," he added, "but he's as good a running back as I've played with."

Over the next several weeks, Davis erased any lingering doubts about his abilities. In the first half alone against San Diego at Mile High, he tore through the defense for 98 yards, then capped his performance by running for 53 yards on Denver's final drive. The Broncos won, 30–27.

The next week, against Jacksonville, he broke the 1,000-yard barrier for the season on his first carry of the game, and went to gain 84 yards for the day. A week later he rushed for 110 yards against Houston, including a 60-yard jaunt. He went over 100 yards for the third time in four games.

With only four games remaining in the season, the Broncos were battling the Chargers for the final spot in the playoffs. As defenses were forced to pay attention to Terrell Davis, quarterback John Elway had more success passing the ball.

But in the Broncos' thirteenth game, against Seattle, Davis's season ended. He injured a hamstring muscle, just as he had done the year before at Georgia. The Denver coaching staff didn't press him to return too early. They knew how valuable he was and wanted to make sure the injury healed completely.

With Davis sidelined, the Broncos lost two of their last three games to finish out of the playoffs with an 8–8 record. Davis was disappointed that the team wasn't playing in the postseason, but he was gratified by his own performance.

He finished the season with 1,117 rushing yards, the lowest draft pick in NFL history to hit the 1,000-yard mark. In addition, he had rushed for seven touchdowns and caught 49 passes, including a touchdown pass, bringing his '95 TD total to eight. He was named the Bronco's MVP on offense, finished second behind New England running back Curtis Martin for the NFL Rookie of the Year, was named to the All-Rookie Team, and was selected as an alternate for the Pro Bowl.

When Terrell Davis saw his name among the league's rushing leaders at the end of the season, on the same list with superstars like Barry Sanders of the Detroit Lions and the Dallas Cowboys' Emmitt Smith, he could hardly believe it.

But he didn't allow his success to go to his head. If he had learned one thing in his young life, it was that everything could change in the blink of an eye — nothing was ever certain. Just because he'd had a good season in 1995 didn't mean he would be a star in 1996. He knew that he'd have to work hard, even harder than before. He realized that as the season had worn on he had gotten tired. He also knew there were times when he didn't pay as much attention as he should have at team meetings. He was now an established player, and his teammates would look toward him to set an example.

He didn't want to let anyone down. He had a lot to improve on.

Chapter Seven:
1996

No Sophomore Slump

In the off-season, Davis was determined to do everything he could to ensure he would not suffer the dreaded "sophomore slump" that affects many players in their second season. He knew that he had sneaked up on the opposition in 1995 and performed above expectations. In 1996, he would no longer be a surprise. Opposing defenses would key on him and do everything in their power to shut him down.

After resting a few weeks, Davis hit the weight room to increase his strength. He also ran nearly every day, doing both sprints and longer runs to build speed and stamina. He consulted with doctors and nutritionists, who gave him advice on what to eat and what supplements to take. He also made arrangements to get a full-body massage several times a week and see a chiropractor on a regular basis to remain flexible and try to stay injury-free. Finally, he did his best to get about twelve hours of sleep each day.

Part of the reason Terrell was so health conscious was his migraine headaches, which bothered him off and on throughout college, and continued when he joined the Broncos. Although he now got only a few migraines each year, he constantly worried that he'd get one on the verge of a game — or worse, in the middle of a game. By taking care of himself, eating healthy foods, and getting the proper rest, he hoped to keep the debilitating headaches at bay. The Bronco training staff helped him with the problem as well and made sure they always had medication on hand whenever he felt a migraine coming on.

When Davis arrived at training camp in July of 1996 for his second pro season, the Broncos were a much improved team. Everyone was more accustomed to Coach Shanahan, and through trades and the draft the Broncos had shored up their perennial weak spot — defense.

Despite the fact that defenses were keying on him, Davis began the 1996 season right where he left off in 1995. He rushed for more than 100 yards in the season opener. Then he did the same against Seattle, and then against Tampa Bay, despite missing more than a quarter against the Buccaneers while he fought off a headache.

The opposition soon realized that Davis wasn't the same runner he'd been in 1995 — he was better! In his rookie year, some had criticized him for lacking the breakaway speed of many of the league's other premier running backs. But after working out hard in the off-season, Davis began to prove his critics wrong.

Against Kansas City on September 22, he exploded for a spectacular 65-yard touchdown romp on his way to 130 rushing yards in the first half alone. The run was the longest of his career. He hadn't even had a 65-yard run in college.

Davis knew why. As he told a reporter, "It dawned on me that at Georgia I got caught because my form broke down. In practice [with the Broncos] we have to run out every play into the end zone. You're used to breaking from the line of scrimmage and then running and running without breaking form."

He was also beginning to master the art of running

in the open field — when to cut back, when to angle to the sidelines, and when to try to fake a defender with a move. He admitted that before 1996, "I didn't do that as well."

When the Broncos played the Baltimore Ravens at Mile High Stadium in midseason, Davis came through with one of the best runs of his career. On the first play of Denver's second possession of the game, from their own 29-yard line, Elway called for Davis to run the ball.

It was a simple off-tackle play, one normally good for only four or five yards. But as everyone was beginning to learn, when Terrell Davis had the ball, he was a threat to score from anywhere on the field.

He took the handoff and burst into the line, exploding into a narrow hole. Spotting a linebacker rushing to fill the hole, he sidestepped him, then accelerated upfield.

As the secondary came up to meet him, he angled toward the sideline. As he was about to be tackled, he stutter-stepped and the defender overran him. In a blink, Davis cut back against the grain toward the middle of the field. When another defender moved in from the opposite side of the field, Davis turned back toward the sideline, taking aim on the orange pylon that marked the front corner of the end zone.

As the crowd roared, he rumbled in for a score. Touchdown Denver! A TD for T.D.! The 71-yard burst keyed another Bronco victory, and Davis went on to rush for a career-best 213 yards.

People now began to say that Davis was not just one of the better backs in the league, he was the best. Against New England in late November, he was almost a one-man team.

The field was muddy and sloppy after a week of rain, poor conditions for most running backs. But Davis wasn't like most backs. Of the Broncos' first seventeen plays of the game, Davis either ran the ball or caught a pass on all but four. The Patriots couldn't stop him, and the result was three quick touchdowns. Denver won, 34–8, as Davis rushed for 154 yards on 32 attempts.

After the game, even the Patriots' curmudgeonly coach Bill Parcells was impressed. "I take my hat off to him," he said of Davis. Bronco tight end Shannon Sharpe was even more effusive. "I don't think there's anyone in the AFC right now who's having a better year." Davis's performance earned him the AFC and NFL Player of the Week awards.

Over the final weeks of the regular season, it seemed as if every time Davis touched the ball he set another Bronco record. He eventually finished the season by establishing team records for rushing yards, with 1,538; touchdowns, with 15; and total carries, with 345. But after streaking to a 12–1 record and clinching the AFC Western Division championship, home-field advantage during the playoffs, and a bye in the first round, the Broncos stumbled. Coach Shanahan rested many of his regulars, and the Broncos dropped two of their last three games to finish 13–3.

They met the Jacksonville Jaguars in the divisional playoff game on January 4, 1997, at Mile High Stadium, where they had gone undefeated all season. With Davis and Elway, the Broncos were the heavy favorite to defeat the Jaguars.

Denver started the game as if they were going to win big. On their second possession, with the game scoreless, Davis broke loose for a spectacular 47-

yard run to set up a touchdown. But the extra-point attempt was blocked.

That didn't seem to matter when Denver got the ball back and marched down the field again, scoring another touchdown on a John Elway pass. They tried to make up for the blocked extra-point attempt by going for a two-point conversion, but failed. Still, Denver led 12–0 at the end of the first quarter. Although Davis suffered a slight injury to a ligament in his knee, one more Bronco score would put the game virtually out of reach.

But the Jaguars didn't give up. The next six times Jacksonville got the ball, they scored three field goals and three touchdowns.

With Davis playing in pain, the Broncos were forced to abandon the running game and go to the air to try to catch up. John Elway brought the Broncos back to within three points when he threw a touchdown pass with just under two minutes left in the game. But the Denver defense was unable to wrest the ball from Jacksonville, and the Jaguars ran out the clock. The Broncos lost, 30–27.

Davis was crestfallen. He knew the team had lost

a game they should have won. He cried after the game, could hardly sleep that night, then woke up in the morning to see his face, in tears, in the Denver newspaper.

Despite running for 91 yards on 14 carries and catching a game-high seven passes for 24 yards, he felt as if he'd let everyone down — his fans, his teammates, even his family. He was embarrassed by the defeat, and hardly left his house for several weeks, emerging only to attend the Super Bowl in New Orleans.

Once there, he soaked up the sights and sounds of the spectacle as Green Bay romped over New England. He wanted to know exactly what he was missing, because Terrell Davis vowed to do all he could in 1997 to make the Broncos one of the two teams playing for the NFL championship. After all he'd accomplished so far in his life, playing in the Super Bowl seemed like the next logical step.

Chapter Eight:
1997

A Super Season

Before the beginning of the 1997 season, the Broncos were picked by many to make it to the Super Bowl — not that they were expected to actually win the game. For while the Broncos had made it to the Super Bowl several times before, they'd never played well in the game. It almost seemed as if they were jinxed.

But Davis wasn't put off by the team's legacy of lackluster performances in the Super Bowl. He felt that this Bronco team was different — and that he was a large reason why.

"I think I could be the difference between past Bronco Super Bowl teams and this team," he told a reporter. "We have a well-rounded team. This is the type of team I look at and compare to past Super

Bowl champions. They [past teams] have a pretty good running game, they have an excellent quarterback, they have good receivers and a great defense, and I think we possess all those things." The presence of a running attack, keyed by Davis, was the big difference.

Davis proved he was willing to do just about anything to help his team. When doctors told him that his poorly aligned teeth might have something to do with his tendency to get migraine headaches, he got braces. He didn't care how they looked.

But just after the beginning of training camp, the Broncos received some bad news. Quarterback John Elway had ruptured a tendon in his right arm. Team doctors expected the injury to sideline Elway for much of the season, if not end his career outright. Without Elway, Denver's championship hopes were considerably dimmer.

Remarkably, however, Elway and the Bronco training staff were amazed to learn that the injury actually allowed him to throw the ball better than he had in the past several seasons. His strong right arm had learned to compensate.

Davis and the Broncos began the season ready to

go all the way. With Davis running and Elway passing, they were almost unstoppable.

During camp, the team's running backs got together to come up with a way to show their solidarity. They decided that each time a back scored a touchdown, they'd give each other a military salute. They started the tradition in training camp and the trademark gesture soon became a favorite among Bronco fans.

In the first game of the season they faced the Kansas City Chiefs, a team many expected to challenge Denver for the conference championship. But Denver's defense shut down the Chiefs and Davis responded with the 11th 100-yard game of his short career. The Broncos beat Kansas City, 19–3.

Terrell followed with another 100-yard effort in a 35–14 pasting of Seattle a week later, and in the third week of the season, against St. Louis, he beat the 100-yard barrier for the third straight time in another 35–14 win. The Broncos were 3–0 and looking invincible.

In the fourth week of the season Davis played one of the most remarkable games of his career. He ran through, around, and over the Cincinnati Bengals for 215 yards, tying the franchise record, and the Broncos cruised to their fourth straight win, 38–20. Davis was named the AFC Offensive Player of the Month for his effort in September.

Although Davis was held under 100 yards for the first time all season a week later against the Atlanta Falcons, Elway picked up the slack and led the team to a 29–21 win. The opposition appeared almost powerless to stop the Broncos. If they tried to shut down Davis by defending against the run, Elway picked them apart. If they tried to protect against the pass, that left plenty of room for Davis to run the football. To keep them off guard, the Broncos mixed it up, using play-action passes. Elway faked giving the ball to Davis, thus freezing the secondary, then passed downfield.

No matter what defense the other team tried to use, Davis dominated. Although the team stumbled and lost to the Raiders in their seventh game of the season, a week later they were back on track.

The team barely made it to Buffalo following a snowstorm that delayed their departure from Denver. They didn't get into town until after midnight.

The next day, for the first time all year, John Elway played a subpar game.

But Davis elevated his game in response. The Broncos just kept giving him the ball and ground out a tough 23–20 overtime win. Davis's game stats were impressive: He rushed the ball 42 times for 207 yards and added five pass receptions for 29 yards, for a total of 236 yards, a franchise record. It appeared as if Terrell Davis might break the single-season NFL rushing record of 2,105 yards set by Eric Dickerson of the Los Angeles Rams in 1984.

Denver ran their record to 9–1 before stumbling a bit. Although the team wasn't helped by a series of nagging injuries to key players, they may have also grown overconfident, just as they had done the previous season.

Their 11–3 record was still good enough to clinch a wild-card berth in the playoffs, but they fell behind the Kansas City Chiefs in the race for the Western Division title. Then, in the next to the last game of the regular season, against San Francisco, Davis suffered a shoulder sprain and was forced from the game. Without him, Denver fell to the 49ers, 34–17.

The Broncos decided to keep Terrell out of their season finale against San Diego to give the injury a chance to heal. They wanted Davis to be both healthy and well rested entering the playoffs. Facing their biggest challenge of the season, they blasted the Chargers, 38–3, to finish the season 12–4, second to the Chiefs.

The injury to his shoulder may have cost Davis a chance to set a new rushing record. Yet despite missing nearly two full games due to the shoulder injury, he still finished the season with 1,750 yards on 369 carries, with 15 touchdowns and 42 pass receptions. But he really didn't care about the record. Now that the regular season was over, all he cared about was getting to the Super Bowl. No wild-card team had ever won the Super Bowl before. But long odds meant nothing to Terrell Davis.

The Denver Broncos earned the right to face their nemesis from 1996, the Jacksonville Jaguars, in the wild-card game in the first round of the playoffs. Coach Mike Shanahan pushed the team in practice all week long, and later said, "We had one of our best weeks. The focus and concentration level was high." The Broncos remembered losing to the

Jaguars in 1996 and they didn't want it to happen again.

Just as they had in 1996, the Broncos jumped out to a quick lead. Winds up to fifty miles per hour swirled through Mile High Stadium, making passing difficult, so the Broncos turned to Davis. He led them on a march down the field on their first possession and bulled into the end zone from two yards out to give his club a quick 7–0 lead.

Denver's defense then shut down the Jaguars. On their second possession, it was Elway who led the Broncos to a score, throwing a long touchdown pass to Rod Smith to make the score 14–0. Denver's defense then held again. With the ball in his hands once again, Davis capped a 92-yard drive with his second touchdown of the day on a five-yard run to put the Broncos ahead, 21–0.

But as in 1996, the Jaguars didn't quit. They scored the next 17 points to draw to within four of the Broncos early in the third quarter. It appeared as if the Broncos were about to blow another playoff game to Jacksonville.

The Jaguars, with first down on the Denver 16-yard line, were on the verge of scoring. But quarterback Mark Brunell fumbled, and the Broncos recovered.

Davis took full advantage of Brunell's mistake. On Denver's second play, he grabbed the handoff, found a hole, and burst through the line. As tacklers bounced off him, he angled toward the sideline and turned upfield. Fifty-nine yards later, he was finally cut down, after refusing to run out of bounds in order to fight for extra yardage. He bruised his ribs on the play and was forced from the game, but the long run got Denver out of a hole and turned the game around. His backup, Derek Loville, ran for two touchdowns and Denver cruised to a 42–17 win.

In only a little more than half the game, Davis had run for 184 yards, helping Denver to a total of over three hundred rushing yards. After the game, he gave his offensive line full credit. "There were some nice holes out there today," he said. "The offensive line just keeps pushing."

The victory set the Broncos up against the Chiefs in the divisional playoff the following week. Although his ribs remained sore, Davis felt good enough to play. Kansas City was favored and had the home-field advantage. He knew his team would need him. Besides, Marcus Allen played for the Chiefs. Davis wasn't about to miss an opportunity to play against the former Lincoln High star.

From the opening kickoff, the game was a defensive struggle. Neither team had much success moving the ball in the first period, and the game remained scoreless until just before halftime.

Then John Elway stepped in. He drove the team down the field in the final minutes of the half, eventually getting a first down on the four-yard line. He handed the ball to Davis. Despite having been held to only 30 yards so far in the half, Terrell scored on a one-yard plunge to put the Broncos ahead, 7–0.

After halftime, the Chiefs came out fired up. They drove down the field before settling for a field goal to start the third quarter, then scored a touchdown late in the period to move ahead, 10–7.

But Denver didn't panic. They stuck with their game plan, which was to use Davis to wear down the Kansas City defense. Davis began breaking tackles and picking up yardage, forcing the Chief defense to focus exclusively on him.

That opened up the passing game. Elway hit receiver Ed McCaffrey on a long pass to the Kansas

City one-yard line. Everybody on the Chiefs and everybody in Arrowhead Stadium and everyone watching the game on television knew what the Broncos were going to do next — give the ball to Terrell Davis.

They were right. Twice Elway handed Davis the ball and twice Davis barreled into the line, trying to score. But the Chiefs dug in and stopped him each time for no gain.

Denver coach Mike Shanahan didn't flinch. He called for Davis to carry the ball a third time.

Terrell didn't disappoint. He burst into the end zone, giving the Broncos a 14–10 lead. Their defense held and the Broncos won.

"Our commitment today shows we're going to run regardless of the situation," said Davis after the game. "We kept running and we wore them down."

They were now only one victory away from the Super Bowl. The only team that stood in their way was the always tough Pittsburgh Steelers. Davis knew it would be a rough game. No running back all season long had rushed for 100 yards against the Steelers.

Both teams started the game a little out of sync.

Elway threw an early interception, then the Steelers missed a field goal.

The Broncos turned to Davis. On the first play of their next possession he dashed around the left end for a 29-yard pickup. Then he ran up the middle for a couple of yards and caught a pass for a few more.

Elway followed with a pass to Ed McCaffrey to the 14-yard line before giving the ball back to Davis. Davis went over left tackle for six yards, and on the next play scampered eight yards around right end for a touchdown. Denver led, 7–0.

Pittsburgh came right back to tie the score, then took the lead with another touchdown. But Elway led the Broncos back, and at halftime Denver led, 24–14.

In the second half, Denver controlled the ball. Time after time, Elway took the snap, spun, and handed the ball to Davis. Though the Steelers were able to keep the Broncos from scoring, in the end, Davis ran through the defense for 139 yards, running out the clock. Despite another touchdown for the Steelers, Denver escaped with a 24–21 victory.

Terrell Davis and the Broncos were going to the Super Bowl!

Chapter Nine:
January 1998

Super in San Diego

Few observers gave the Broncos much of a chance against the defending Super Bowl champions, the Green Bay Packers. Led on offense by Pro Bowl quarterback Brett Favre and on defense by legendary end Reggie White, the Packers were a tough and experienced team. Green Bay had blown out the New England Patriots in Super Bowl XXXI, 35–21, and was favored to repeat as champion.

In comparison, the Broncos looked weak. For despite Elway and Davis, no one thought their undersized offensive line could match up against the massive Packers. In addition, their opportunistic defense was considered only a little above average.

But John Elway made the Broncos sentimental favorites. After fourteen years as one of the top quarterbacks in football, all he lacked to complete his career was a Super Bowl victory. Terrell Davis and his teammates were resolved to help him reach that goal.

This year's Super Bowl had special meaning to Davis, for it was scheduled to be played in his hometown, San Diego, at Qualcom Stadium. He would have dozens of friends and family members in the stadium for the game, and his brother Reggie was throwing a huge Super Bowl party at the house they all grew up in.

The week before the game, Davis was honored at Lincoln High. He attended a ceremony where they retired his jersey. He was a hero at his old school, for everyone there knew just how far Davis had come and how much he had overcome to make it in the NFL.

But nothing had ever come easily to Terrell Davis, and that proved true at the Super Bowl as well. For on the day of the game, as he prepared to play the game of his life, one more unexpected obstacle stood in his path.

He prepared for the Super Bowl the way he got ready for every game — listening to music, getting taped, and putting on the parts of his uniform in a particular order. But in the excitement, he forgot to do one very important thing. On the advice of doctors, he always took medication about an hour before the kickoff to help prevent a migraine headache. In fact, ever since he'd started taking the medication, he'd never been bothered by a migraine.

But on this day, he forgot to take his medication. When he remembered ten minutes before the start of the game, he quickly swallowed a pill — and tried not to worry.

At first, it didn't seem to matter whether Davis had a migraine headache or not. Green Bay took the opening kickoff and marched smartly down the field as Brett Favre picked apart the Bronco secondary. Only four minutes into the game Favre threw a touchdown pass to Antonio Freeman to give the Packers a 7–0 lead.

Bronco fans all over the country looked at each other in dismay. Every previous time the Broncos had reached the Super Bowl, they'd been blown out early. Falling behind so soon to the explosive Green Bay team appeared to be a bad omen.

But Denver returned the ensuing kickoff to their own 42-yard line, then started giving the ball to

Davis. He ripped off two four-yard runs, then caught a pass for another four before Elway threw three incompletions. Fortunately for the Broncos, Green Bay was penalized for holding, and Denver got a first down.

Thinking Denver would pass, Green Bay's aggressive defense decided to blitz to try to sack Elway. But the Broncos crossed them up.

As the Packers charged forward, Elway spun and handed the ball to Davis. The Denver line opened a hole. Davis charged past the blitzing Packers before they knew what was happening. All of a sudden, he was in the clear.

As the secondary approached, Davis broke for the left sideline. Proving once again that he had more than enough speed to make it in the NFL, he galloped down the field for a 27-yard gain before being tackled. The Broncos had the ball on the Green Bay 14-yard line.

After a gain of two yards, Elway scrambled for a first down. Two plays later he gave the ball to Davis again. Davis did not let the team down. He roared into the end zone. One kick through the goal posts later, the game was tied.

Green Bay quickly turned the ball over on an interception, and Denver took possession just past midfield. Davis ran for 16 yards on the first play, and soon Denver was knocking on the door of the end zone again.

From the Green Bay ten-yard line, Davis crashed over the right tackle for a five-yard gain. But he was hit hard on the tackle, and Packer end Santana Dotson inadvertently hit him in the head with his knee.

Everything went black. Davis was conscious, but the blow induced a migraine. He sat on the ground for a moment, unable to see.

On television, the announcers speculated that Davis was groggy after the hard tackle. Calling for an injury time-out, Denver's trainer raced onto the field to see what was wrong with him.

Davis struggled to get control. After a few moments, his vision cleared slightly. He was able to stand up and walk off the field amid cheers from the thousands of fans watching — fans who questioned whether Davis would make it back into the game anytime soon.

Terrell answered their question moments later. When the ball was put back into play, he jogged onto the field. He didn't want to let his team or the fans down.

Elway fed him the ball again, and although Terrell was nearly blind, he pounded down to the Packers' two-yard line. Then, fortunately, the gun went off signaling the end of the first quarter.

Davis made it back to the sideline as the Bronco staff huddled, planning their next move. The Denver trainer gave Davis a special nasal spray used to treat migraines and told Coach Shanahan that his running back would be all right. "It should clear up in another ten or fifteen minutes," the trainer said.

But the Broncos couldn't wait ten or fifteen minutes. They couldn't afford to miss an opportunity to score. Shanahan approached Davis and asked how he felt.

Davis was panic-stricken. "I can't see," he blurted out to his coach, "I can't see."

Shanahan paused for a moment, then spoke softly to his young star.

"Okay," he said. "Just do this. We're gonna fake it to you on a Fifteen Lead. But if you're not in, they won't believe it." The play called for Elway to fake a handoff to Davis, then run a bootleg around the right end.

Davis just nodded, pulled on his helmet, and gingerly ran onto the field. Denver huddled, then lined up. Elway barked out the signals, took the snap, and spun around.

The Packers had no idea that Davis couldn't see. They fully expected the Broncos to give him the ball and surged forward to stop him. Moving from memory, Davis ran forward with his arms apart. Elway stuck the ball into his midsection then pulled it away. Davis wrapped his arms around the imaginary ball, put his head down, and ran forward into the Green Bay line.

None of the Packers noticed that Elway still had the ball until it was too late. Elway danced around the right end and scored a touchdown without a single Packer laying a finger on him. Davis gave Elway a weak salute, then stumbled toward the sideline, his head pounding. Denver led, 14–7.

The trainer gave him some more nasal spray.

Davis promptly threw up. Then the trainer clamped an oxygen mask over his face. Davis covered his head with a towel to block out the light that made the pounding in his head even worse. Coach Shanahan took one look at his star running back and told the trainer to take him to the locker room.

Davis lay down on a bench in the cool, quiet locker room throughout the second quarter. He could still hear the crowd's distant roaring. The Broncos scored on a long field goal by Jason Elam, but Green Bay came right back. Just before halftime Favre drove his team the length of the field and threw a touchdown pass to Mark Chmura with only seventeen seconds left to play. The Broncos charged off the field at the half nursing a narrow 17–14 lead.

In the locker room, Davis's teammates offered him words of encouragement. As the team rested for the second half, Davis's medication finally began to take effect. When they went out to start the second half, Davis was back to normal.

Or so he thought. For on the second play of the half, with the ball on his own 26-yard line, he took the ball and, while fighting for extra yardage, fumbled. Green Bay recovered.

Davis felt terrible but assured his teammates his gaff had nothing to do with how he felt. He'd just lost control of the ball and promised them it wouldn't happen again.

The Bronco defense got him off the hook. They stopped the Packers cold, and Green Bay had to settle for a field goal to tie the game.

The two teams exchanged possessions, then Denver got the ball back again. Mixing passes by Elway and runs by Davis, they moved down the field. But at the Green Bay 16-yard line, the drive threatened to stall.

On third down, Elway drifted back to pass. Denver desperately wanted to score a touchdown, but all the receivers were covered. The quarterback rolled out to the right side, avoided a tackle, and set his sights on the first-down marker. He was hit so hard his body was launched into the air. Amazingly, he held on to the ball, and when he landed he was on the ten-yard line. First down.

Elway's gutsy play fired up his teammates. They turned to Davis to punch the ball into the end zone. This time there was no need to fake a handoff. He was ready.

The play resulted in a short gain. On second down, Elway handed him the ball again and the Denver line exploded from the blocks. They blew the Packers off the line and Davis danced through an enormous hole off-tackle, scoring the touchdown without even being touched. He was swarmed in the end zone by his teammates and freed himself only to salute everyone. Denver was back in the lead, 24–17.

But Green Bay refused to give up. Early in the fourth quarter, Favre took the Packers 85 yards in only four plays and knotted the score.

There was only one thing for the Broncos to do: Keep Favre off the field and run some time off the clock. The best way to do that was to give the ball to Terrell Davis.

As hoped, he chewed up time as they marched down the field. They didn't make it into the end zone, but neither did the Packers when they finally got the ball back.

Then, with just over three minutes left, Denver took possession at midfield. The game was on the line.

Davis ran twice, the Packers were penalized for

holding, and Elway completed a 23-yard pass to full-back Howard Griffith. Suddenly, the Broncos had the ball at the eight-yard line. Davis nearly scored on the next play, but a penalty pushed the Broncos back to the 18-yard line.

Davis got the ball again. He rumbled 17 hard yards to the one. With less than two minutes to play, a touchdown could give the Broncos a victory.

There was no better player in the league to power the ball into the end zone than Terrell Davis. He plowed over the line and gave the Broncos a 31–24 lead.

Green Bay desperately tried to score, but failed. Denver took over and ran one last play. John Elway downed the ball and the whole team watched as the clock ticked off the final seconds of the game.

The Broncos won! Quarterback John Elway grabbed Davis and kept yelling, "T.D.! T.D.!" over and over. On the public address system, Davis heard that his 157 yards rushing and three touchdowns, all in only three quarters of play, had earned him the Super Bowl MVP award. He could hardly believe it.

When the team returned to their hotel for a postgame celebration, Davis simply went to his room and met with his family and a few close friends. He was happy, but completely exhausted. While the rest of the team partied long into the night, Terrell Davis went to bed early.

His dreams had all come true, and now all he wanted to do was go to sleep.

Chapter Ten:
1998

A Super Return

Davis's superb Super Bowl performance vaulted him into the national spotlight. Over the next few weeks he made a number of television appearances and received requests to endorse a variety of products as corporations scrambled to have the humble running back serve as their spokesman.

Davis turned down most of the offers. He didn't want to cheapen what he had accomplished or lose his focus for the upcoming season, although he did agree to serve as a spokesman for the company that made his migraine medication.

In recognition of his achievements, the Broncos tore up his existing contract and rewarded him with another, more lucrative one. The new contract made him financially secure. It also gave him the opportunity to start giving something back. He'd worked hard for what he had achieved, but he still felt fortunate. He wanted to give others the same opportunity.

He set up several charitable foundations, including the Terrell Davis Salute the Kids Foundation, to help kids reach their dreams, and the Terrell Davis Migraine Foundation, to raise awareness of treatment for migraine headaches. He also worked with sportswriter Adam Schefter to write his autobiography, entitled *TD: Dreams in Motion.*

But Davis spent most of the off-season following his usual routines, working out hard and making sure he got the proper rest. Although his performance in the Super Bowl had made him famous, as far as he was concerned, his career was just beginning. There was still more he wanted to do on the football field, and he kept his distractions to a minimum.

His commitment was infectious. When the Broncos arrived at training camp for the 1998 season, they weren't satisfied to relive the previous season's triumphs. They wanted to win the Super Bowl again. They knew if they did they would be considered one of the greatest teams of all time.

Although many had speculated that quarterback John Elway would retire following the Super Bowl win, he decided to return. But even with Elway, Davis and the Broncos knew their task in 1998 would be even harder than it had been in 1997. As defending champions, they'd have the toughest schedule in pro football. Every team they played would be looking to knock them off.

It seemed impossible, but once the regular season began, Terrell Davis was even better than he had been in 1997. After being held to only 75 rushing yards in the Broncos' first game, against New England, he ripped off an incredible seven straight 100 yard–plus performances, including 191 yards against the Cowboys and 208 yards against Seattle. His strong running opened up the field for the passing game, and the Broncos were undefeated.

Two of the NFL's most hallowed records seemed within reach. Davis was on pace to break Eric Dickerson's single-season rushing record of 2,105 yards set in 1984, and the Broncos looked unbeatable. If they went through the regular season undefeated and won their second consecutive Super Bowl, they'd match the record of the 1972 Miami Dol-

phins, the only team in NFL history to go undefeated for an entire season.

But Davis and the Broncos eventually learned just
how difficult it would be to reach those milestones.
With a record of 13–0, the Broncos played the
defensive-minded New York Giants.

Although Davis bounced back from two straight
sub-100-yard performances by rushing for 147
yards, New York dumped the Broncos, 20–16. Their
chance for an undefeated season was gone. Then, a
week later, a fired-up Miami Dolphin team smoked
the Broncos, 31–21, and held Davis to only 29 yards.
Davis entered the final game of the season needing
more than three hundred yards to set a new record,
an impossible task.

But, more important, the Broncos desperately
needed a win. Their two-game losing streak had
rattled the team and they'd lost momentum. They
needed a win against Seattle to build their confidence for the playoffs.

Davis restored their faith. He rushed for almost
two hundred yards and the Broncos blasted the Sea-
hawks, 28–21. Although Davis failed to set a new
single-season rushing record, he still finished the

season with 2,008 yards, becoming only the fourth player in NFL history, along with Dickerson, O. J. Simpson, and the Detroit Lions' Barry Sanders, to rush for more than 2,000 yards in a single season.

He was rewarded by being named the NFL's Most Valuable Player and becoming the only unanimous choice for the Pro Bowl team. The awards were nice to have, but not what he really wanted.

His team's 14–2 record in the regular season simply put Davis in position to reach his real goal — another Super Bowl win. The team took advantage of their bye in the first week of the playoffs to shake off nagging injuries, rest, and prepare for their title defense.

The Miami Dolphins beat the Buffalo Bills in the AFC wild-card game, 24–17, to earn the right to play the Broncos. If they beat the defending champs, the Dolphins would be one step closer to the Super Bowl. Like the Broncos in 1997, the Dolphins were the sentimental choice of many fans to win the Super Bowl. The reason was Dolphin quarterback Dan Marino.

Like Elway, Marino had been a star in the NFL since entering the league in 1983. And like Elway,

Marino had won every award imaginable, but never the Super Bowl. Now that Elway had his Super Bowl victory, many fans wanted the same thing for Marino. The Dolphins were confident after their victory over Denver in the regular season, and many observers were predicting an upset.

But someone forgot to tell that to Terrell Davis. He remembered how he'd been shut down a few weeks earlier and was determined not to let it happen again.

In the first quarter, he scored two touchdowns to put Miami down, 14–0. Forced to play catch-up, the Dolphins had to turn to the pass. Denver's defense harassed Marino to the point of distraction. Meanwhile, Davis just kept plugging away, chewing up yardage in huge chunks, gaining 199 yards on only 21 carries. The Broncos won big, 38–3.

"It was a personal challenge to play better this time," Davis said after the game. "I give the offensive line all the credit."

John Elway then stated the obvious: "He's the best in the business and maybe the best there ever was." Mike Shanahan added simply, "He did it all today."

One week later, he did it again. Playing the rugged New York Jets in the AFC Championship Game, Davis led a Denver comeback after New York opened up a 10–0 lead. He rushed for 167 yards on 32 carries as the Broncos scored 23 unanswered points to win, 23–10. "As the game went on, they got tired," he speculated later of the Jets' poor second-half performance.

The Broncos had earned the right to return to the Super Bowl. In the NFC, the surprising Atlanta Falcons beat the Minnesota Vikings. Led by running back Jamal Anderson and quarterback Chris Chandler, the Falcons were brimming with confidence. They relished the chance to dump the favored Broncos.

But the Broncos were ready to defend their title. Rumors abounded that John Elway was going to announce his retirement after the game. He'd slowed considerably during the season, even sitting out several games with injuries he'd once have been able to play through. If it was to be Elway's last game, Davis and his teammates were determined to do whatever they could to give him a proper send-off.

Atlanta took the opening kickoff of Super Bowl

XXXIII in Miami and drove for a field goal. Then the Broncos got the ball.

Elway was sharp from the very beginning and, with help from Davis, moved the Broncos quickly down the field. With a 14-yard pass completion to Shannon Sharpe, the team had a first down on the Falcons' one-yard line.

Atlanta knew what to expect next. They'd spent the last two weeks analyzing the Broncos and knew that Davis was almost certain to get the ball.

But Coach Mike Shanahan had expected the Falcons to key on Davis. In response, he decided to cross them up. Instead of giving the ball to Davis, he called for fullback Howard Griffith to run the ball.

Griffith, although a good runner, didn't get many chances to carry the ball. He usually blocked for Davis. But when he got the ball on the play, he knew what to do with it. He crashed into the end zone to put Denver ahead, 7–3. For one of the few times all season long, Davis was on the receiving end of the touchdown salute. He didn't mind at all.

The two clubs exchanged several possessions before John Elway demonstrated why many considered him the best quarterback in NFL history. After

Atlanta missed a short field-goal attempt, Denver took over at the 20-yard line.

With the Falcons keying on Davis, he was used as a decoy once again, faking a run on a play-action pass. As Davis surged into the line, Elway faded back and hit receiver Rod Smith in stride. Smith streaked downfield and into the end zone. The 80-yard touchdown and point after gave Denver a 14–3 lead.

The Falcons couldn't recover. Later in the game, Davis served as a decoy for a third time as Griffith scored on another short touchdown run. After Elway scored with just over eleven minutes remaining in the game, Denver had an insurmountable 31–6 lead.

The Falcons tried to come back and managed to score twice in the final minutes. But Davis did his job in the final quarter, running out the clock and finishing with 102 rushing yards. The Falcons just couldn't compete. The Denver Broncos won their second consecutive Super Bowl, 34–19.

Although John Elway was named Super Bowl MVP, everybody knew that Terrell Davis had keyed Denver's undefeated run in the playoffs. His 468 rushing yards in the postseason was the third highest total ever, and his total of 2,476 yards rushing in the regular season and postseason combined broke his own record of 2,331 set in 1997.

After the game, Davis admitted that he'd suffered from cramps almost the whole game. "I knew it was going to be tough," he said. "Every time I took a step or two, I was locking up."

But that didn't stop him. Nothing ever did. Terrell Davis was absolutely determined to do whatever he could to help his team win. After all he'd been through to reach this point, cramps were nothing.

Asked to compare the two Super Bowl victories, he didn't hesitate to answer. "This one is a lot better," he said. "Last year was a good one, but to go through the season having to play every game and trying to get back is tough."

But not nearly as tough as playing against Terrell Davis, the most determined man in football. "I didn't mind being a decoy at all," he added. "It doesn't matter. I'll do whatever I need to help this team win championships."

Spoken like a true champion.

Matt Christopher

Sports Bio Bookshelf

Terrell Davis

John Elway

Julie Foudy

Wayne Gretzky

Ken Griffey Jr.

Mia Hamm

Grant Hill

Randy Johnson

Michael Jordan

Lisa Leslie

Tara Lipinski

Mark McGwire

Greg Maddux

Hakeem Olajuwon

Emmitt Smith

Sammy Sosa

Mo Vaughn

Tiger Woods

Steve Young

MATT CHRISTOPHER

The #1 Sports Writer for Kids

Read them all!

All available in paperback from Little, Brown and Company

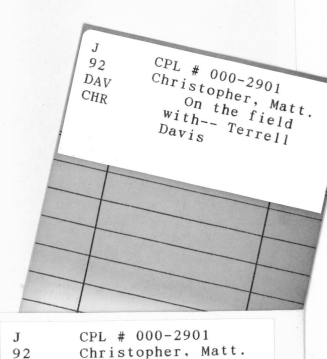